ARTIST ARCHIVES™ INTRODUCTION BY MAX ALLAN COLLINS

PIN-UP NUDES II

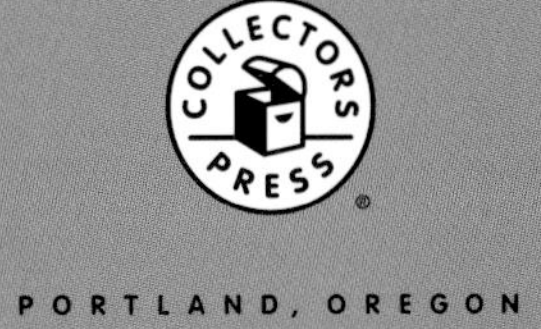

PORTLAND, OREGON

PIN-UP

NUDES II

Art Direction Principia Graphica
Design Hoover H.Y. Li
Editor Ann Granning Bennett

The artwork contained herein is from the archives of Collectors Press, Inc. We are always seeking to expand our collection. If you are interested in selling your pin-up originals or ephemera please contact Collectors Press, Inc.

Printed in Hong Kong

Library of Congress Cataloging-in-Publication Data
Pin-up nudes II / introduction by Max Allan Collins.
p. cm. -- (Artist archives)
ISBN 1-888054-57-3 (alk. paper : pbk.)
1. Pinup art--United States. 2. Female nude in art. I. Title: Pin-up nudes 2. II.Title: Pin-up nudes two. III. Collins, Max Allan. IV. Series.
NC1878.E7 P56 2002
760'.04424'0973--dc21 2001008385

First American Edition

9 8 7 6 5 4 3 2 1

FOR A FREE CATALOG WRITE TO COLLECTORS PRESS, INC.

P.O. Box 230986
Portland, Oregon 97281
Toll Free 800-423-1848
Or visit our website at *www.collectorspress.com*

INTRODUCTION

FOR THE MOST PART, when masters of "pin-up" art such as Rolf Armstrong, Gil Elvgren, and Earl MacPherson, among others, depicted a fetching female subject, the image and atmosphere became a naughty next-door neighbor to Norman Rockwell's *Saturday Evening Post* world of Mom, apple pie, and the family dog.

Part of that was a peculiarly American fantasy, one that really seemed to blossom in the later Depression years, flowering during World War II and immediately thereafter: that the-girl-next-door, whether in petticoats or booby sox, might be a siren rivaling any Broadway beauty or Hollywood starlet; that Mom once might have been a chorus girl; that the family dog once twisted a leash around shapely female limbs, exposing silk stockings.

These future homemakers were surreptitiously seen in scanty, yet socially acceptable attire – sunsuits, bikinis, négligées – and they wore fashions that showed off but did not boast about their figures, waiting instead for a breeze to lift a skirt and produce evidence. Prior to this, artists often used the pretense of historical, mythical, and Biblical settings (particularly in the pre-pin-ups of the 1920s and 1930s) – Cleopatra and Delilah were sex goddesses justified by antiquity. Or illustrators invoked exotic settings where Indian maidens and South Sea Islands girls could be excused for their pagan pulchritude.

But in the Golden Age of the Pin-up – the 1930s through the early 1950s, a glorious period ushered in by Rolf Armstrong, George Petty, Alberto Vargas, and Gil Elvgren – such pretentions were cast aside for contemporary settings, often contriving to place modern young women in compromising positions.

Scratch any commercial artist, however, and find beneath the surface an artist who once aspired to Fine Art or, anyway, schooled in disciplines conducive to that supposedly nobler path. These artists were, obviously, trained students of anatomy. So, now and then – not as often as you might think, largely due to social constraints – the pin-up artists abandoned their kitschy props and their models' skimpy costumes to fashion nude studies.

Often the pin-up artists would try to achieve an aura of Fine Art, of classical aspiration, to get away with delineating an undraped girl-next-door. Even in the most prudish of times, the widely published portrait of a beautiful nude – "September Morn," in which a maiden covered herself modestly, wading in waters dappled with morning sunlight – bedecked calendars, candy boxes, cigar bands, and postcards. After all, "September Morn" – exhibited in the Paris Salon of 1912 by painter Paul Chabas, winning a Medal of Honor – wore the seal of approval of Fine Art; if da Vinci and Michelangelo depicted nude female subjects, why not Rolf Armstrong or Gil Elvgren?

Still, nude calendars were then – as now (witness *Playboy*'s yearly array of naked Playmates – relegated to all-male bastions such as barber shops, fraternity houses, and lodge halls. Though marketed over the counter now, nude calendars are not designed for public display; as I wrote in the first collection of these nudes, even a garage banished these bare beauties to back walls.

Only in recent years – through the efforts of pin-up enthusiasts, including Art Aimsie, Charles Martignette, and myself – that Elvgren has been elevated to a position alongside Alberto Vargas and George Petty. From a purely nostalgic point of view, Elvgren outshines either of those masters, whose pin-up girls existed in a fantasy world of wealthy bachelors, reaching a primarily affluent audience, at least until "Varga" calendars were circulated to servicemen.

Elvgren, on the other hand, saw his work displayed in those aforementioned barbershops, frat houses, and lodge halls, where his stunning oils of heartbreakingly beautiful girls-next-door – dresses blowing up over lovely, lithesome legs – subliminally connected with an audience familiar with the wholesome Coca-Cola Santa Clauses of his mentor, Haddon Sundblom.

Elvgren (1915-1980) contributes to our cover image, "Bewitching," paying tongue-in-cheek homage to Fine Art conventions. The chair, the lace fan, the thorny roses add a still-life aspect to a voluptuous central subject who has arrayed herself in an extremely unlikely manner (what is she doing?). The brushwork invokes both old masters and Rockwell, even as the fan coyly obscures nipples, and the painfully symbolic thorny roses discreetly mask any public hair. Art-study trappings or not, the lush lipstick and the pile of blonde hair are pure pin-up.

Elsewhere in these pages, Elvgren's "Modern Venus" is another bold combination of Fine Art clichés and outright pin-up girl. Flowers and fabrics and a ponytailed subject present a more natural pose than "Bewitching," the sly humor has been replaced here by the pure romance of an obviously young model who projects a sunny innocence not always found in Elvgren's girls.

The father of the American pin-up, Rolf Armstrong (1889-1960), is represented by the classically title "Venus." Armstrong rose to fame in the Roaring Twenties, and he often depicted bedroom-eyed flappers-next-door. His idealized Clara Bow-ish beauties appeared not only as calendar girls, but on magazine covers and sheet music, his drowsily sensuous young vamps often emerging from vivid swirls of color.

"Venus" is an atypical subject, if a typically lovely work of art, by the man who introduced pastel as a major pin-up medium. Petty worked in artbrush with Vargas, Merlin Enabnit, and others following. Elvgren followed his master Sundblom in oils, thereby inspiring a cadré of his own imitators. But Armstrong inspired countless artists, including wonderful ones such as Earl Moran, Zoë Mozert, and Earl MacPherson (all on display in these pages). The shimmeringly beautiful blonde of Armstrong's "Venus" is a girl-next-door all right, radiating sex appeal even as she transcends it. Small-breasted, leggy, lovely, "Venus" perfectly bridges the pin-up and the art-study nude.

The most successful Armstrong acolyte, Earl Moran (1893-1964), did not directly imitate his role model; he contributes "Reflection" to this volume, a work of art any museum might covet. To the end of his life, Moran – a master of pastels who occasionally worked in oil – painted subjects that boldly combined the Fine Art and pin-up approach. Some of his loveliest of these studies – like "Reflection" – were masterpieces of light and shadow, Moran cloaking his naked beauties in darkness, not skimpy clothing. This approach – the nude's radiant flesh glimpsed in darkness – was ideal for pastel and became a sub-genre Moran and Zoë Mozert dominated.

Iowa-born, the prolific Moran studied at the School of the Art Institute of Chicago and went from advertising clients to calendar giant Brown & Bigelow, becoming one of its biggest names. He created pert, playful pin-up girls who willingly shared their beauty without teasing. Moran also successfully entered the field of magazine illustration (*Life*), sold Hollywood movie posters (*Something for the Boys*, 1944), and co-published a "girlie" magazine, *Beauty Parade*, contributing occasional covers. His most enduring pin-ups feature Marilyn Monroe, who, as Norma Jean Baker, had been his model in the late 1940s.

The most famous pin-up artist, Zoë Mozert (1907-1993), offers up her own variation on Moran's "Reflection" with "Tranquility," an astonishingly beautiful work whose blue and orange-red palette invokes Maxfield Parrish. Moran and Mozert, with their tasteful, evocative studies of nudes in darkness, exemplify the Fine Art nude pin-up.

Mozert's "Bubbles" is another matter entirely. As boldly as Elvgren, Mozert presents a pin-up subject in a typical provocative pin-up pose and situation, sans clothing. Few pin-ups are as lushly beautiful as this one, frankly erotic, and yet the blonde subject is so matter-of-fact in both her beauty and nudity, nothing salacious is conveyed.

Other than her own model, Mozert rejected sexy-girl clichés to depict more real-seeming young women, individual in their features and personalities. Her cover portraits of Hollywood starlets for *Romantic Movie Stories*, *Screen Book*, and other magazines were enormously popular. The majority of her work – including many more nudes than any other pin-up artist, with the possible exception of Moran himself – was calendar-oriented (primarily for Brown & Bigelow). But Mozert also made an impact as a movie-poster artist, notably with the infamous Howard Hughes/Jane Russell sex-and-saddle saga, *The Outlaw*. Even her less sultry sirens convey both charm and sex appeal.

Other major pin-up talents provide examples of their best work in these pages. Armstrong's most shameless imitator, Billy DeVorss (1908-1985) serves up "Such a Little Lamb," an inexplicable pose enhanced by the artist's typical romanticism. Frequently posing live models, DeVorss – largely self-trained – worked in pastels, the medium of his idol Armstrong (even DeVorss's signature was an imitation of the great Rolf), and his beauties often similarly displayed dazzling smiles and sleek limbs. Still, DeVorss had his own special charm – his works, however uneven, exude warmth, his subjects radiating a good-natured sexuality and the promise of romance.

Earl MacPherson (1910-1993), the king of sketchbook artists (sketchbooks pretended to be pages ripped from the artist's pad) tenders us the most traditional pin-up in this book, without any pretense of a Fine Art approach, in his untitled portrait of a blonde bubble dancer whose twin balloons (so to speak) reflect a brunette "fellow" chorine. Meanwhile, MacPherson's sketchbook rival K.O. Munson gives us "Lovely to Look At," a pensive pose that displays the artist's adroitness in pastel, one of the few pin-ups here that tips the scale closer to Fine Art.

Walt Otto (1895-1963) offers up "Lovely Lady," one of the most striking, boldest nudes herein. Otto is another proponent of Elvgren-esque oils-on-canvas, creating beaming American beauties in a lush, Sundblom-esque brushstroke style. Despite his painterly technique, he varies considerably from the romanticized hyper-realism typical of the Sundblom/Elvgren school; Otto's paintings often exhibit cartoonier elements, most notably in the expression of his winsome girls. Even Otto's signature might be that of a cartoonist.

Also, Otto's women are seldom as coy as Elvgren's; usually outfitted in a bathing suit or short shorts, Otto's beauties stare unabashedly at the viewer. Often, Otto uses a Petty-style grease-pencil line as shorthand for a dog leash or a phone cord, abandoning any suggestion of background and using a solid color to better focus the attention on the pretty subject at hand.

But in "Lovely Lady," Otto invokes a Fine Art approach in the draped table the blonde leans against, and his model's gracefully rendered figure – however improbably long-stemmed – certainly makes for an admirable nude study. What is most remarkable, however (and yet typical of Otto), is his subject's unashamed, brash gaze at the admiring observer. Her bedroom eyes seem to stare into a more brazen sexuality of decades to come.

These nudes remain a relative rarity from the Golden Age of Pin-up calendars, partly due to the purity of the times. Even so, most of these artists – being at heart illustrators who liked to tell a story – preferred to present a situation (often a compromising one) in which a pretty girl could show off her charms...even if that did mean painting a few clothes on her.

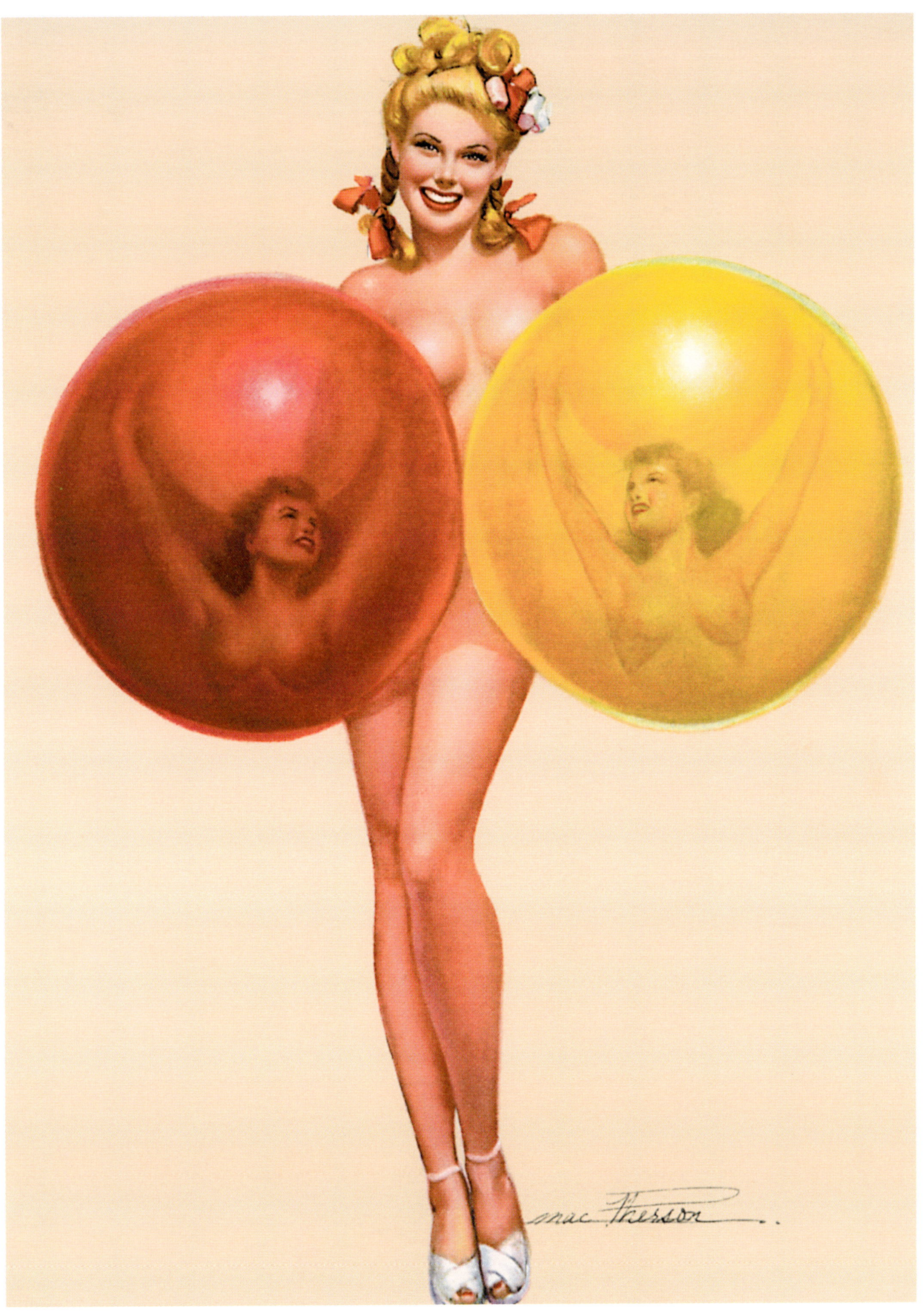
mac Pherson

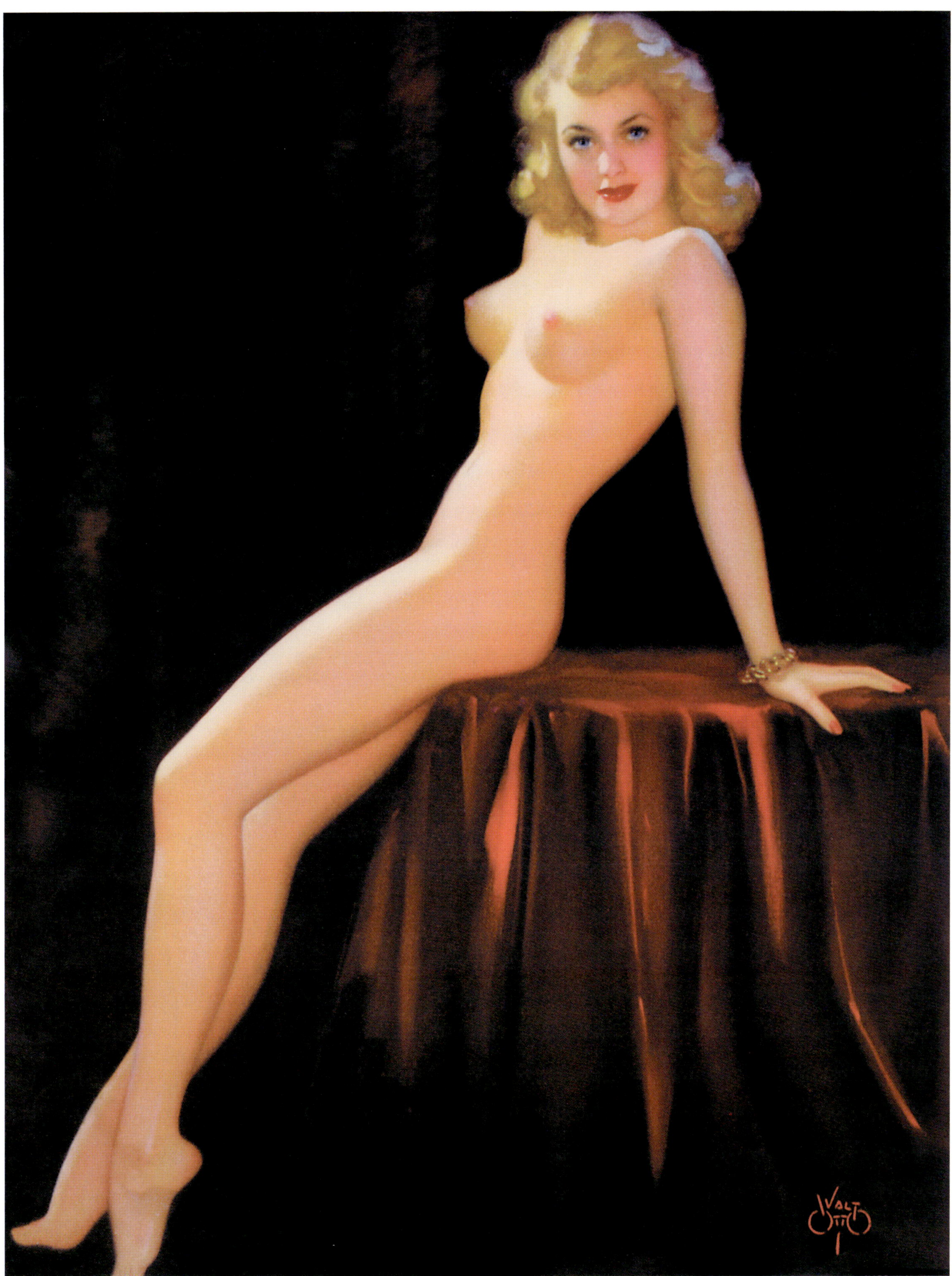

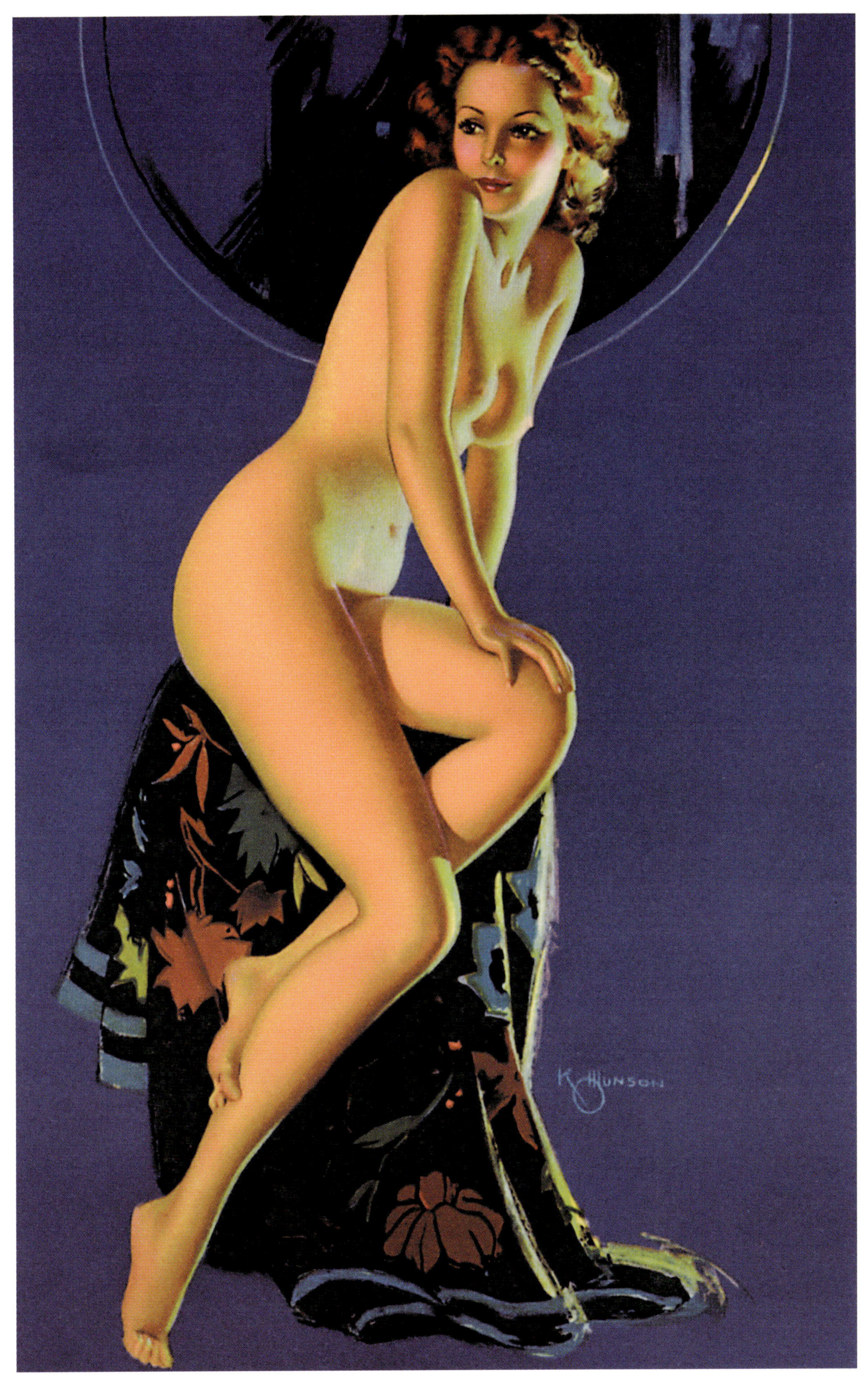
K. MUNSON

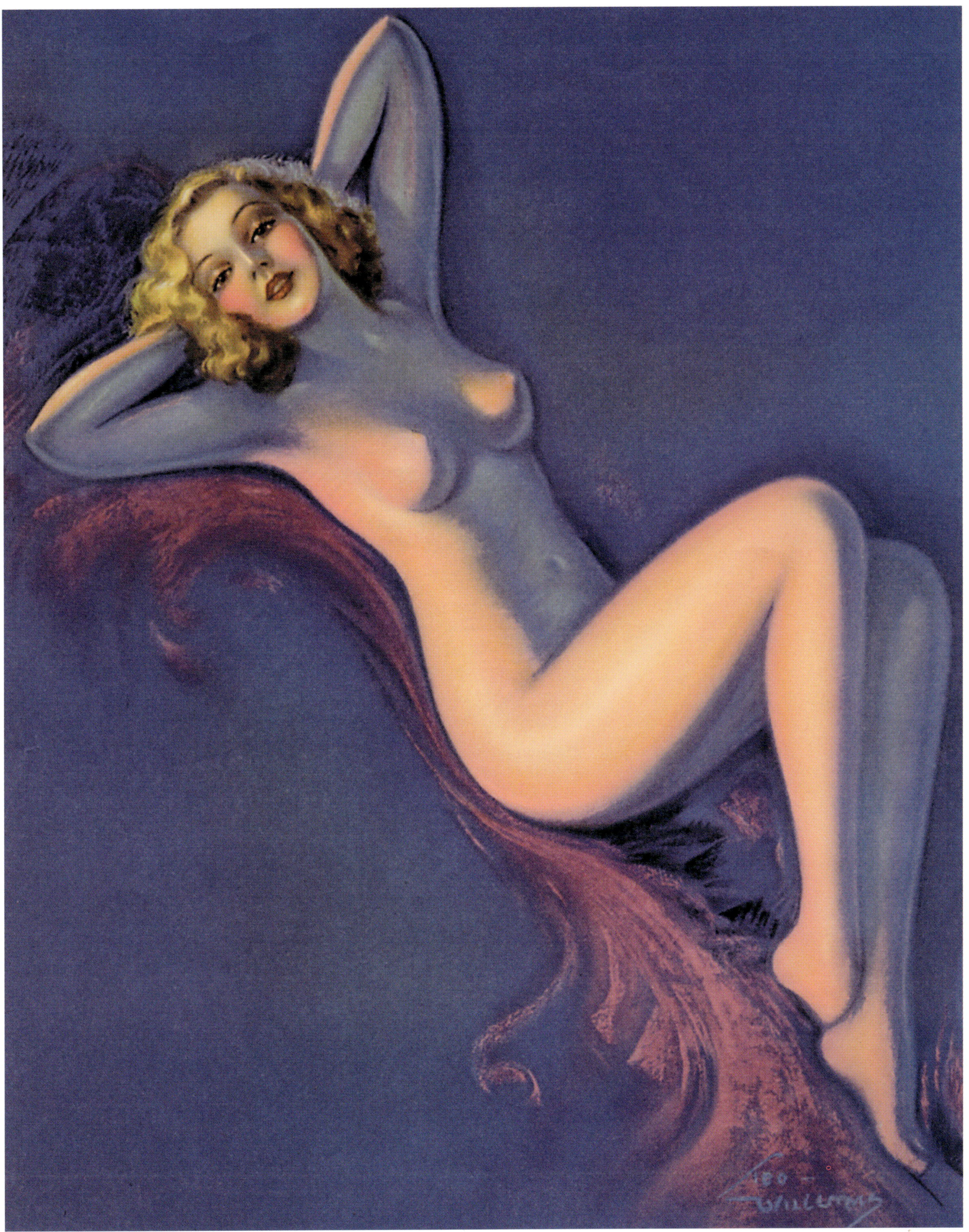

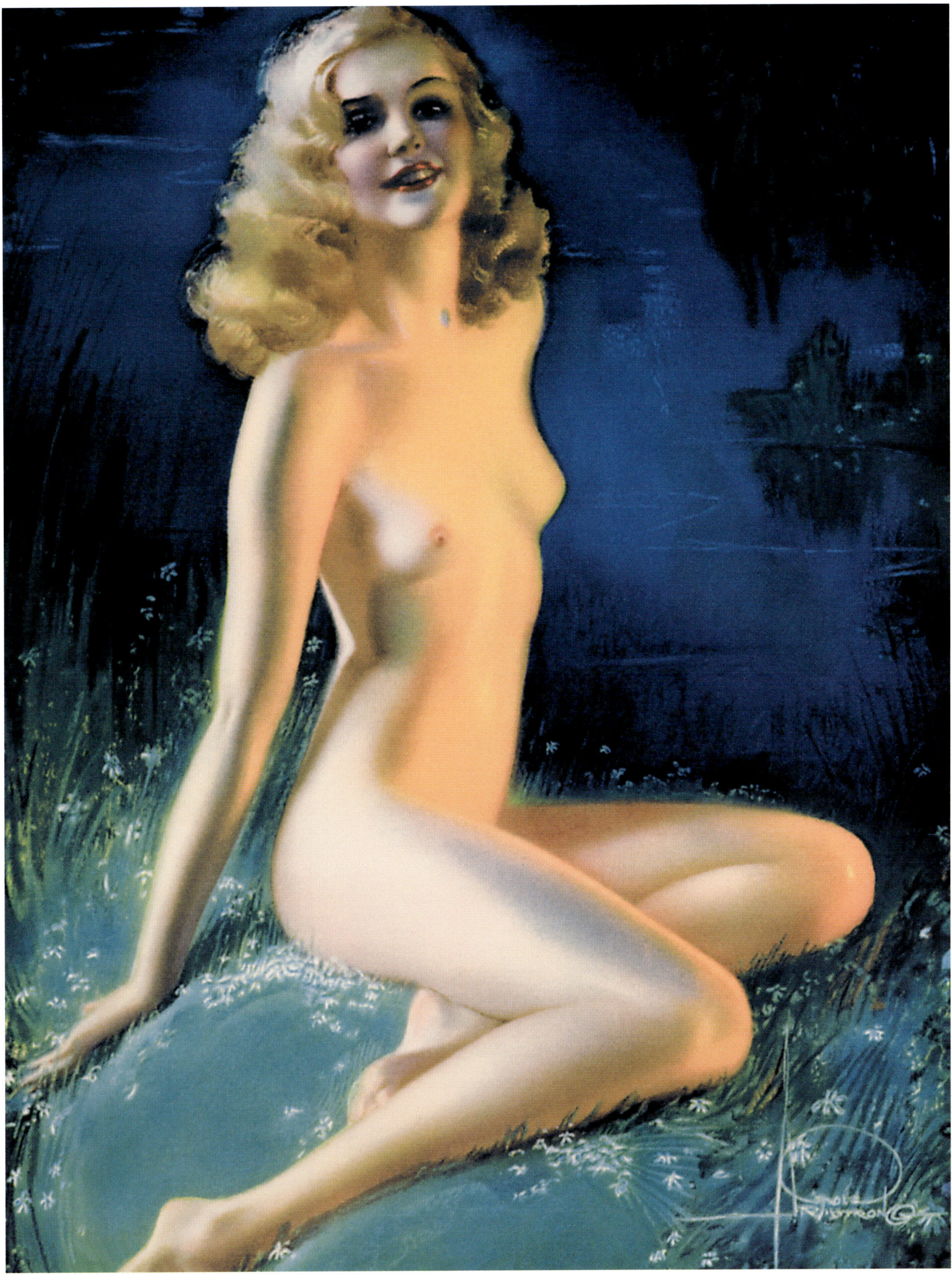

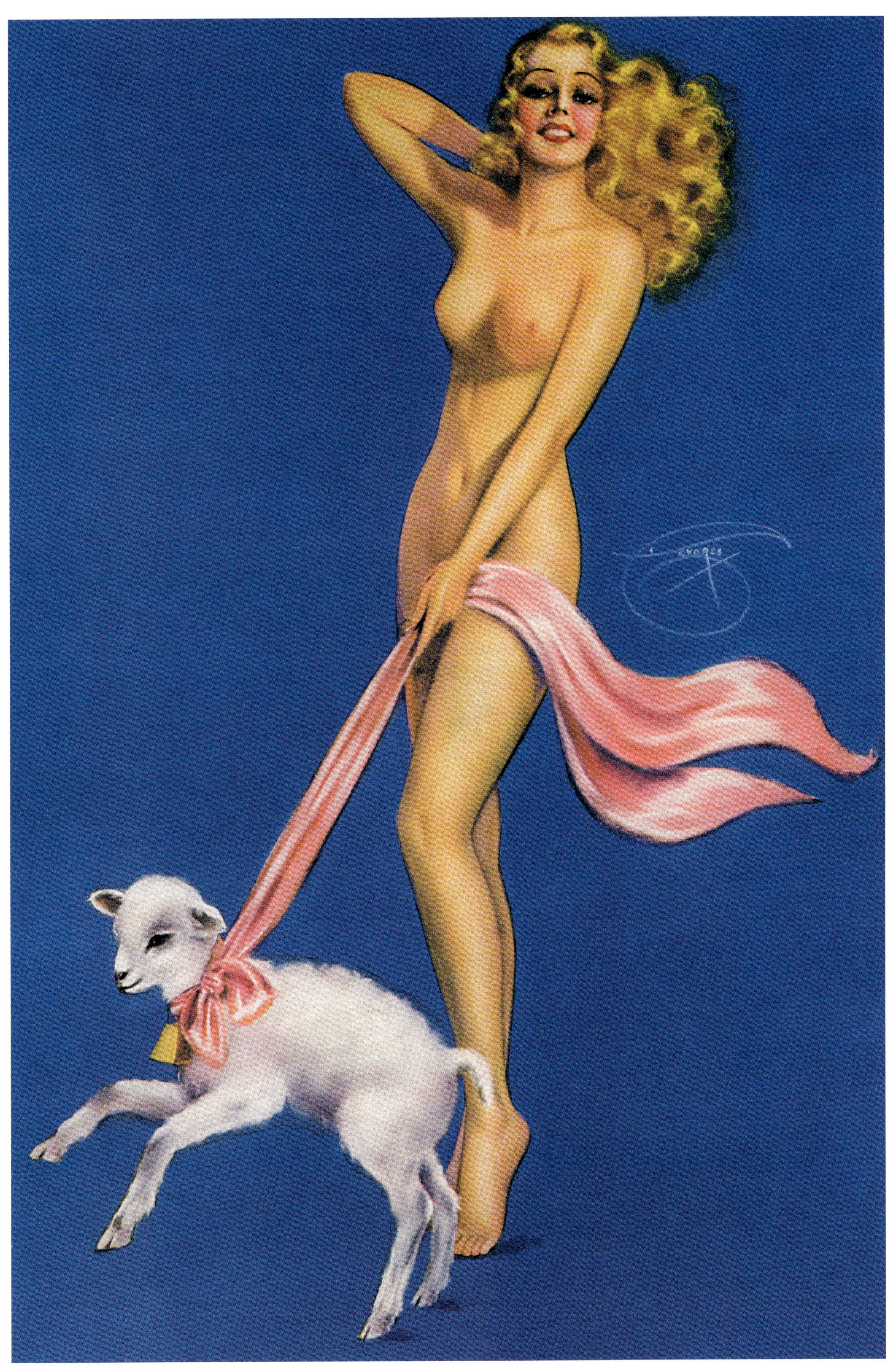

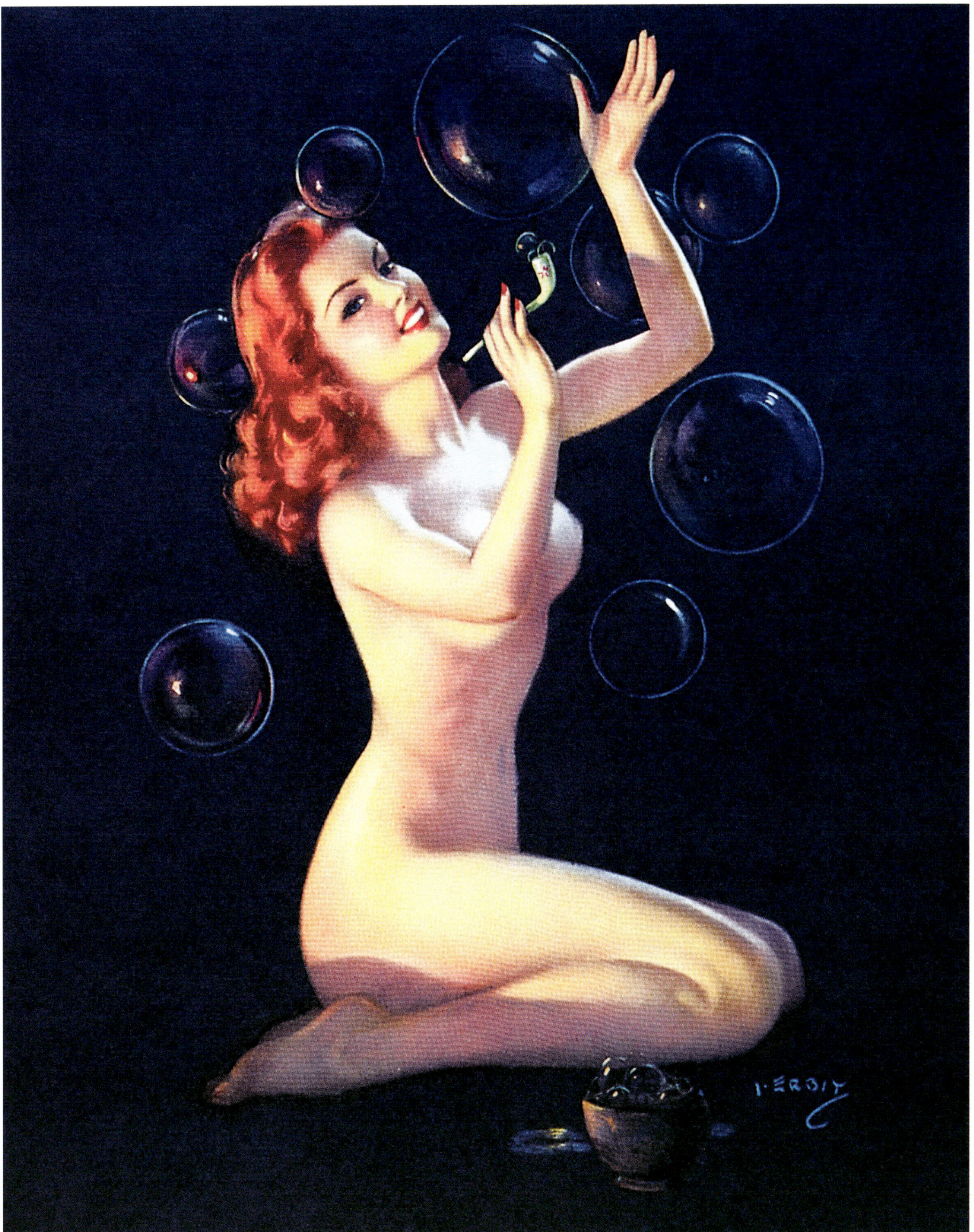

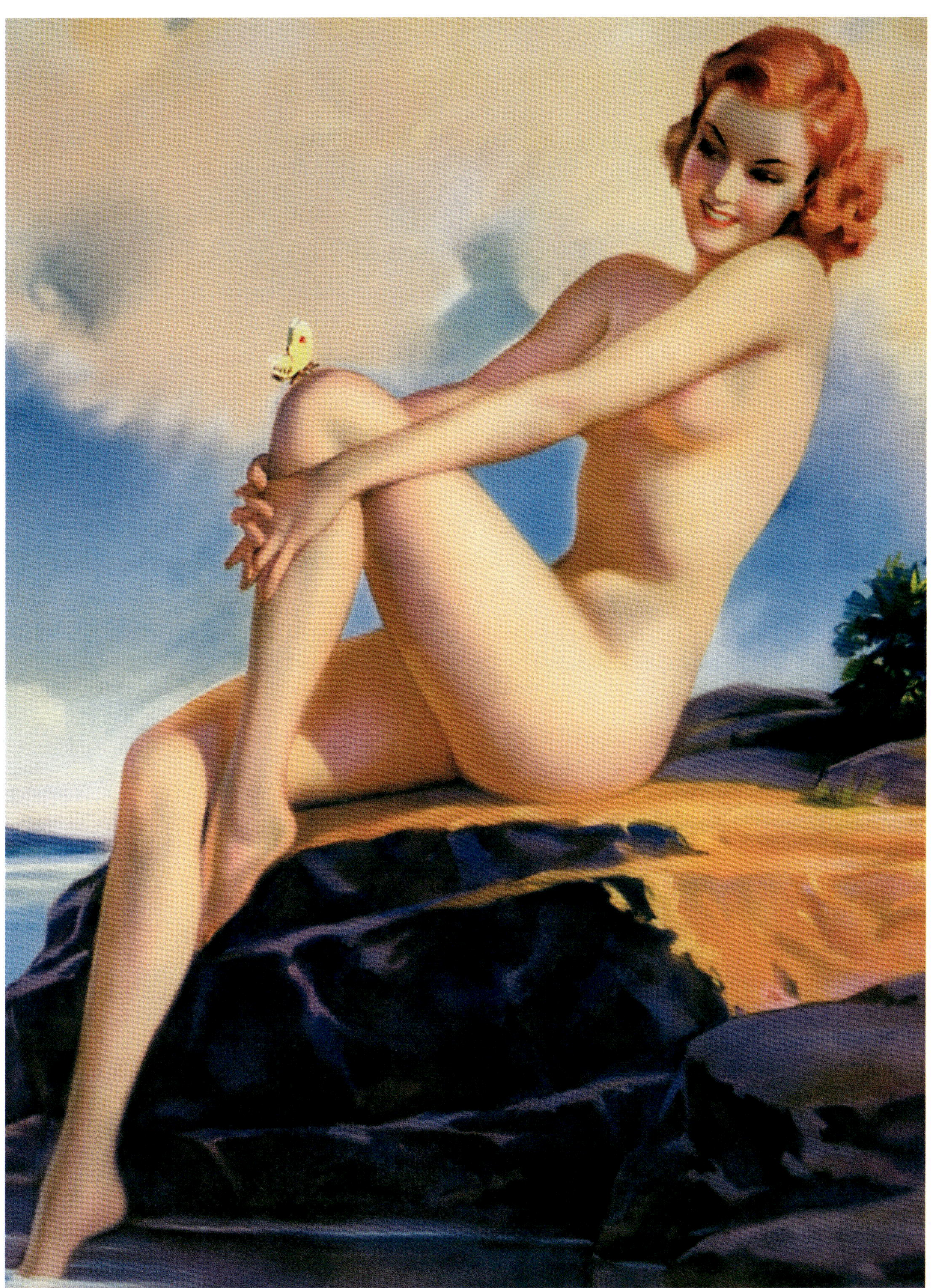

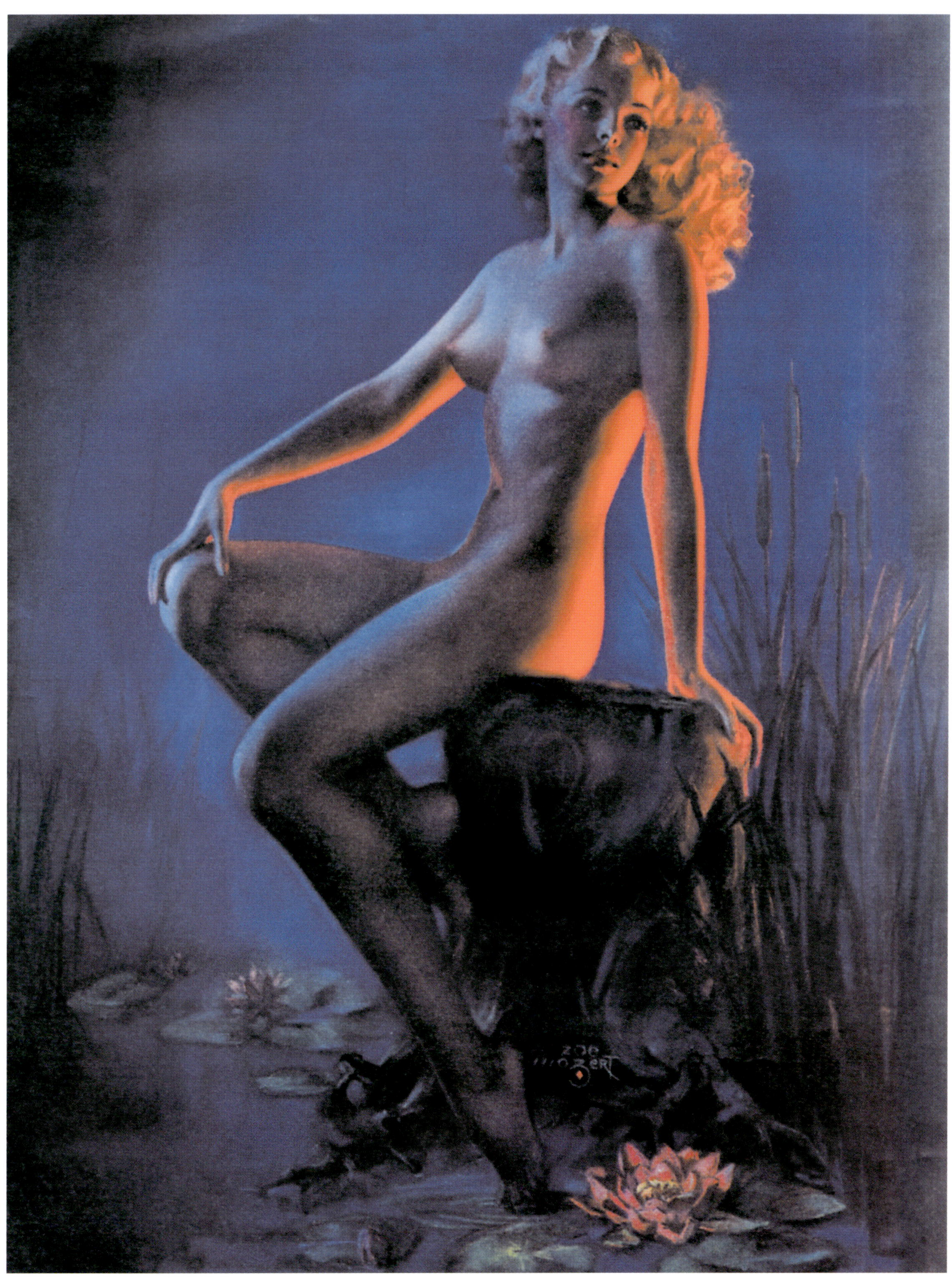
ZOE
MOZERT

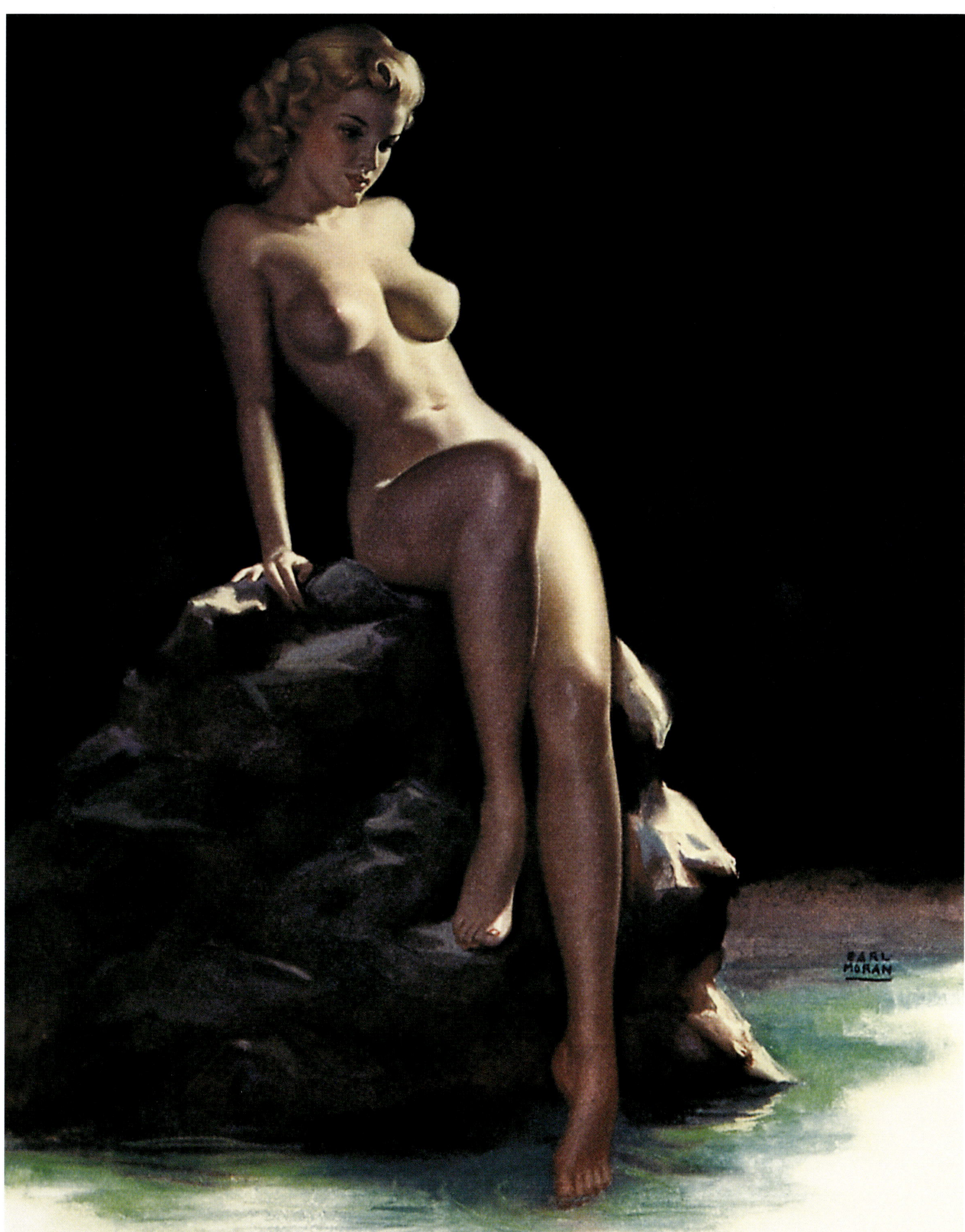
EARL
MORAN

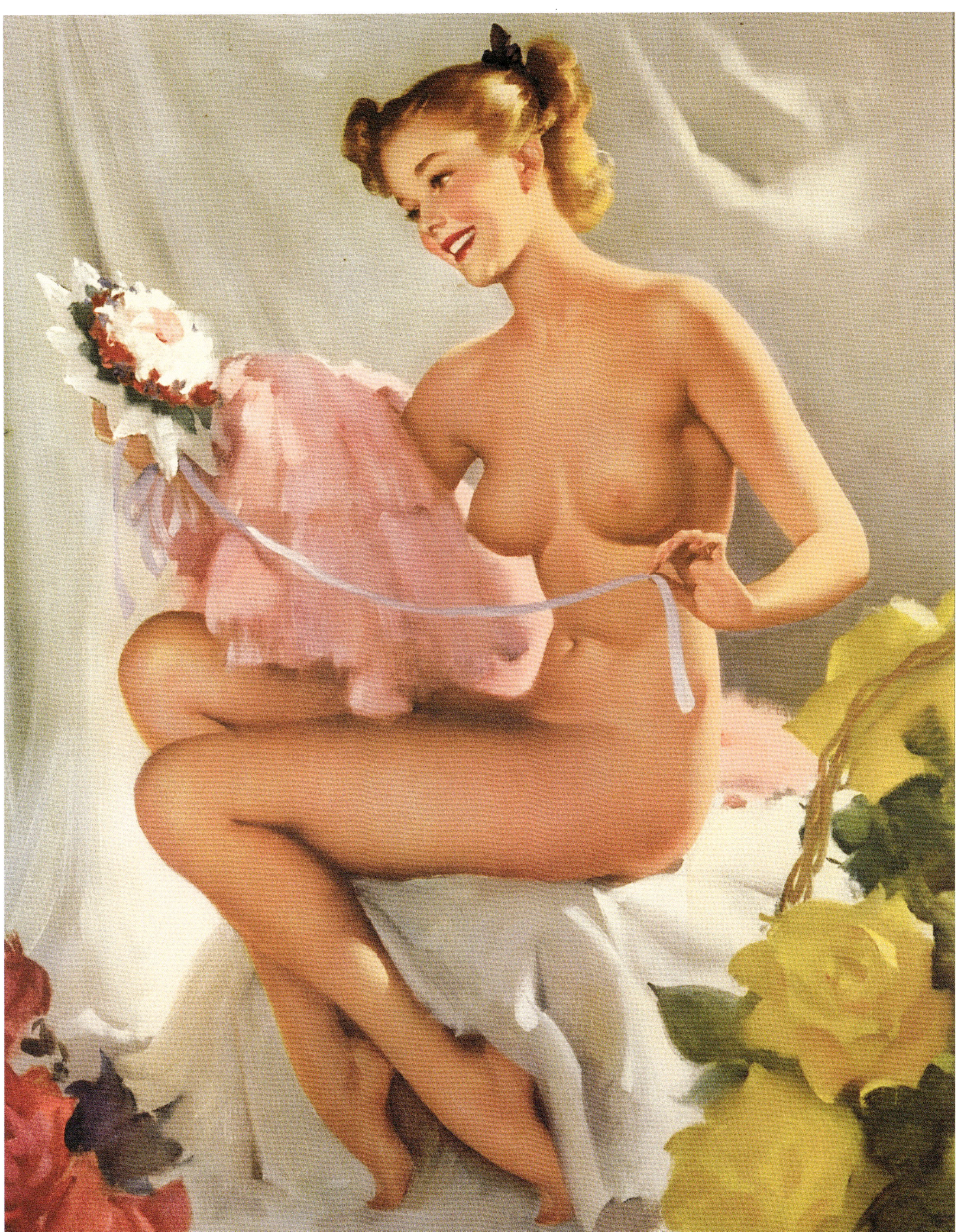

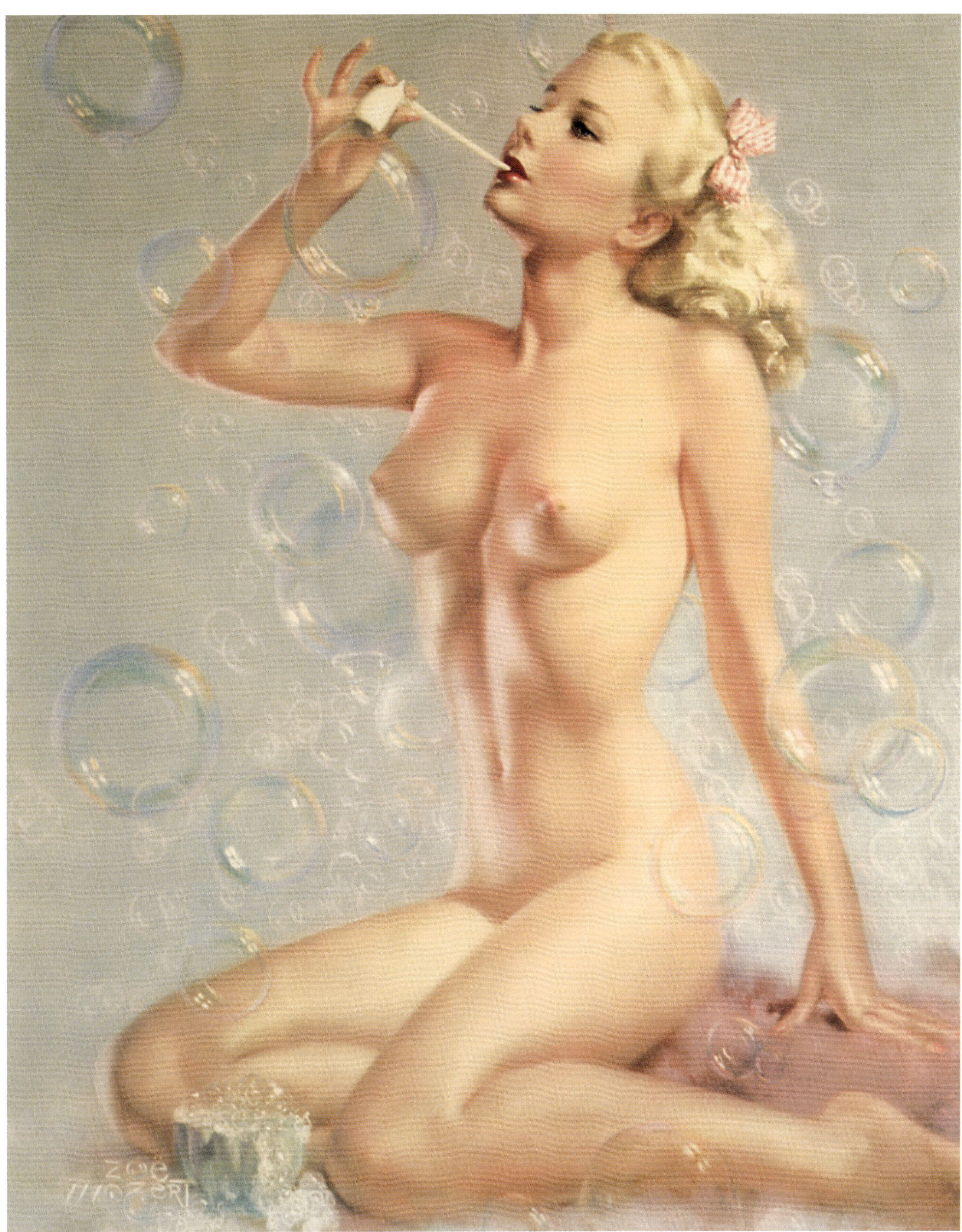
ZOË
MOZERT

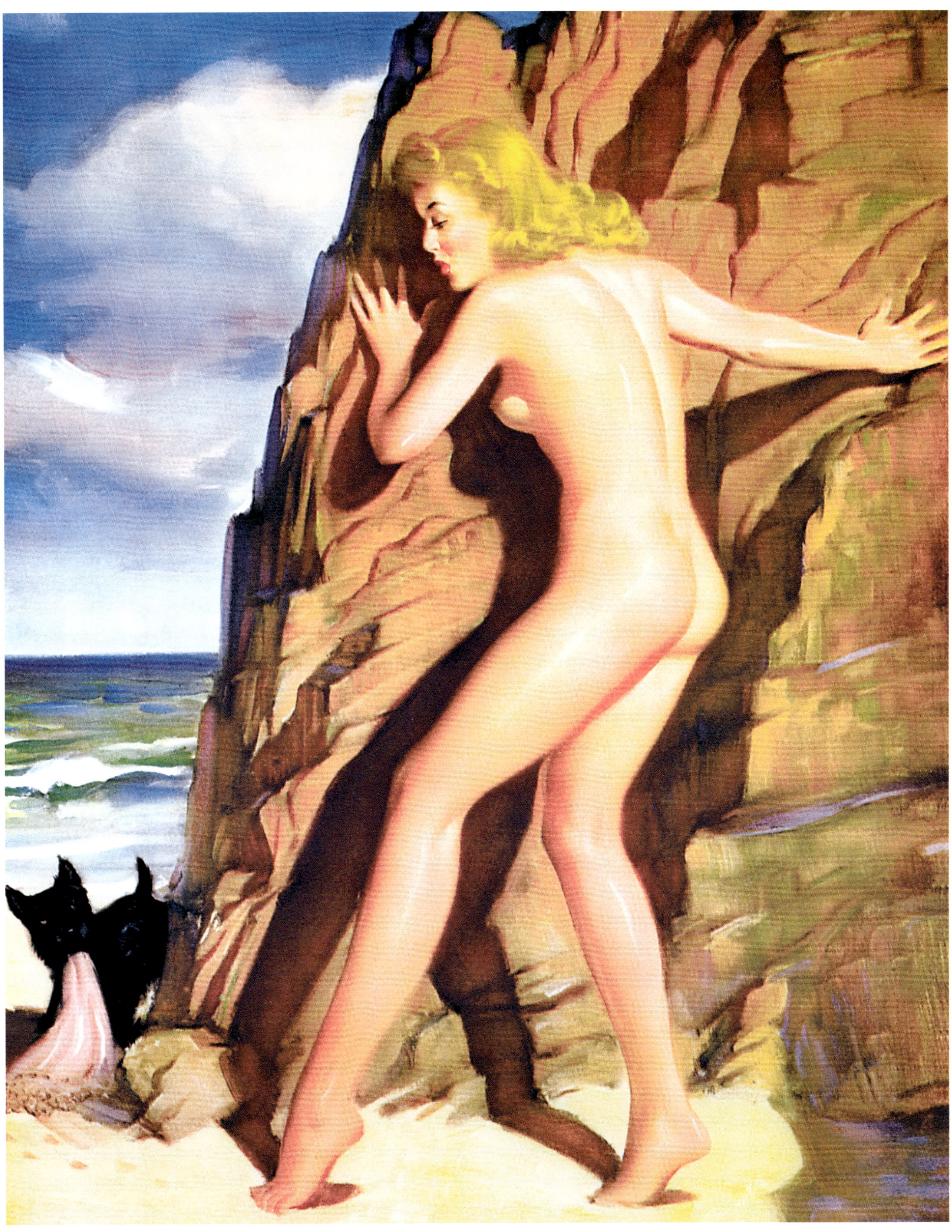

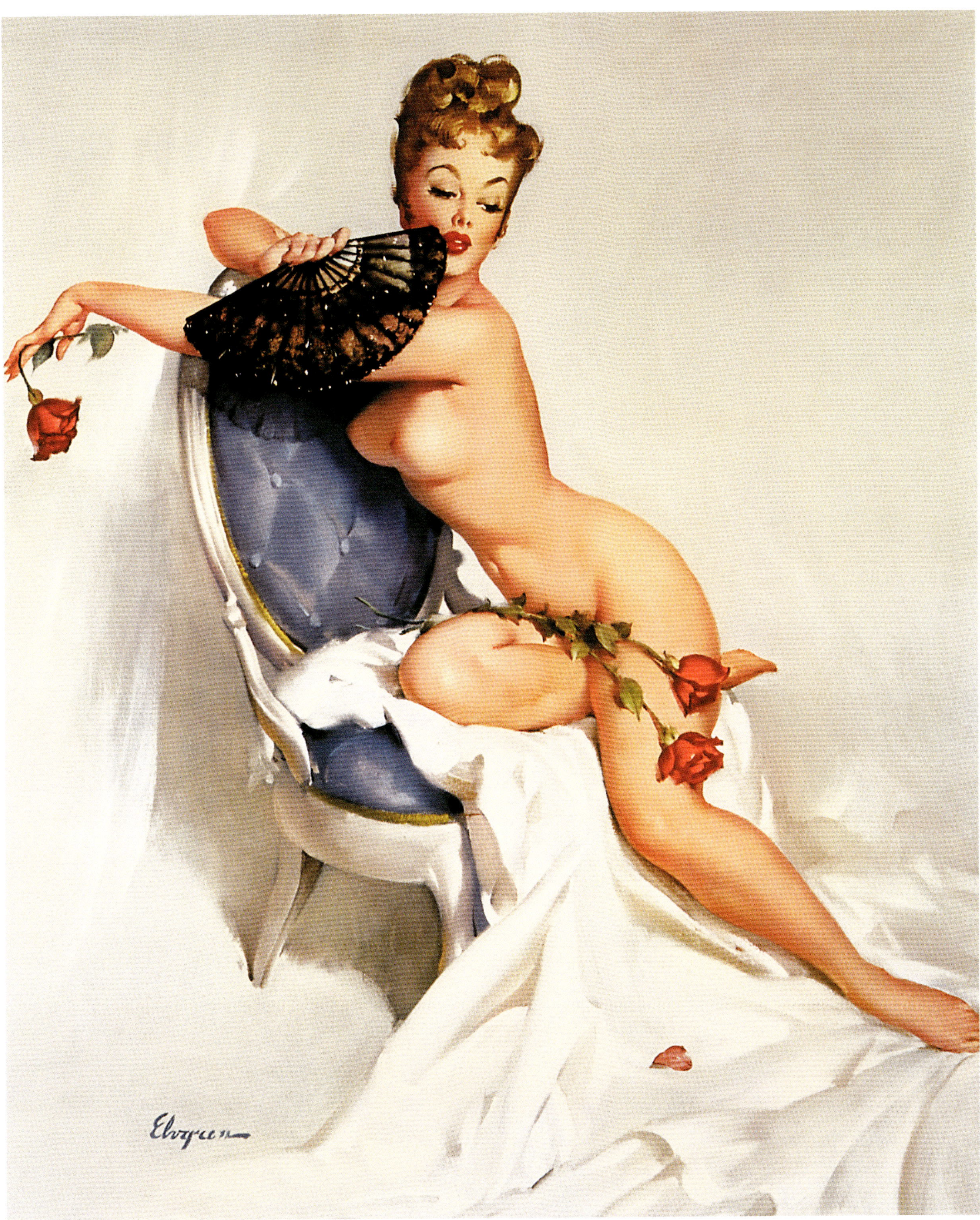
Elvgren